Life in the West

TERESA DOMNAUER

Children's Press®
An Imprint of Scholastic Inc.
New York   Toronto   London   Auckland   Sydney
Mexico City   New Delhi   Hong Kong
Danbury, Connecticut

Content Consultant
David R. Smith, Ph.D.
Adjunct Assistant Professor of History
University of Michigan
Ann Arbor, Michigan

Library of Congress Cataloging-in-Publication Data

Domnauer, Teresa.
Life in the West / by Teresa Domnauer.
    p. cm.—(A true book)
Includes bibliographical references and index.
  ISBN-13: 978-0-531-20583-9 (lib. bdg.)   978-0-531-21246-2 (pbk.)
  ISBN-10: 0-531-20583-5 (lib. bdg.)   0-531-21246-7 (pbk.)

1. Frontier and pioneer life—West (U.S.)—Juvenile literature. 2.
Pioneers—West (U.S.)—History—19th century—Juvenile literature. 3.
Pioneers—West (U.S.)—Social life and customs—19th century—Juvenile
literature. 4. West (U.S.)—History—1860-1890—Juvenile literature.
I. Title. II. Series.

  F596.D66 2010
  978—dc29   2009014184

1 2 3 4 5 6 7 8 9 10 R 19 18 17 16 15 14 13 12 11 10   62

Find the Truth!

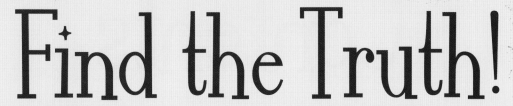

Everything you are about to read is true *except* for one of the sentences on this page.

Which one is **TRUE**?

T or F   The pioneers were the first people to settle the American West.

T or F   Some early Western homes were made from dirt and grass.

Find the answers in this book.

Contents

Pioneers used nets to scoop grasshoppers off their crops.

Wagon trains headed west from eastern parts of the United States.

CHAPTER 1

A Land of Hope

In the mid-1800s, thousands of people were traveling across the United States to the West. Some were searching for gold. Others wanted to practice their religion freely. Still others hoped to own land and find a better life for their families. Their journey by covered wagon was long and hard. Many travelers did not survive the trip. The determined **pioneers** who did make it gradually settled the wild lands west of the Mississippi River.

About 500,000 settlers traveled west on routes that included the Oregon Trail.

Lewis and Clark were helped by different tribes of Native Americans during their journey through Louisiana Territory.

Blazing New Trails

In 1803, the United States bought a large area of land west of the Mississippi River from France. This deal was called the Louisiana Purchase, and it doubled the size of the United States. President Thomas Jefferson hired army captains Meriwether Lewis and William Clark to explore the area. Fur trappers, or hunters, and traders also ventured through this region. All of these explorers paved the way for others to move west.

The Oregon Treaty

Both Great Britain and the United States wanted to own land in the West. They were each interested in the Oregon region. In 1818, the two countries agreed to share this area. By 1846, thousands of American settlers were living in the region. That year, Great Britain chose to give up its **claim** and sign the Oregon Treaty. This agreement stated that Oregon would now belong to the United States.

This map of the United States shows the areas of the West that were under the control of other countries.

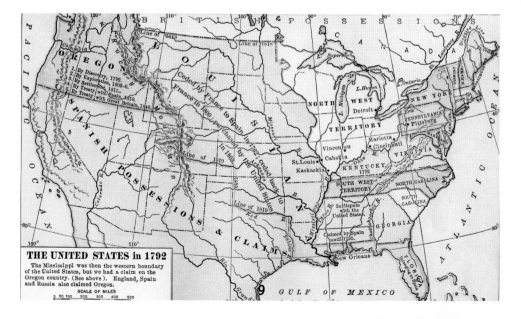

THE UNITED STATES in 1792

The Mississippi was then the western boundary of the United States, but we had a claim on the Oregon country. (See above). England, Spain and Russia also claimed Oregon.

SCALE OF MILES
0 50 100 200 300 400 500

9

Going for the Gold

A man named James Marshall was one of those Americans who moved west. In 1848, while working at Sutter's Mill, California, he discovered gold. A year later, the California gold rush was on. News of it spread quickly around the world. Thousands of people traveled to California in hopes of getting rich. They came from as far as Europe and South America. With all of these people in the West, cities, businesses, and farms grew quickly.

Gold seekers called piles of dirt containing bits of gold "pay dirt."

When people made improvements to their land and gained ownership, it was called "proving up."

The Homestead Act

In the 1860s, the east and west coasts of America were crowded with people. Many of these people wanted more open space where they could own land. To make this possible, Congress passed the Homestead Act in 1862. For a small fee, any U.S. citizen could buy 160 acres (65 hectares) of land between the Mississippi River and the Rocky Mountains. After working the land for five years, these settlers could legally own it.

African Americans were among the
many pioneers who settled the West.

CHAPTER 2

A Place for All People

Many formerly enslaved African Americans went west to find better lives. **Immigrants** (IH-muh-grints) from around the world journeyed there, too. Some wanted to escape from wars in their countries. Others wanted to own land or practice their religion freely. As these new settlers traveled west, they met many Native Americans whose people had lived on the land for centuries.

The Homestead Act allowed many former slaves to own land for the first time.

Immigrants from Across the World

After the Homestead Act was passed, many settlers arrived in the Great Plains (a huge grassy area stretching from Texas to Canada) and the West. The U.S. government also advertised these areas to Europeans. The ads offered affordable farmland. This brought many Europeans to America.

Many men from China also moved to the American West. They worked as miners and railroad builders. Some Americans **discriminated** (diss-KRIM-uh-nate-id) against the Chinese because they did not understand their ways of living.

Chinese immigrants called California Gum Saan, which means "gold mountain."

14

An African American family in front of their Kansas home

African Americans

In 1865, the U.S. government passed the
Thirteenth Amendment to the Constitution.
This amendment, or law, made slavery illegal.
Once African Americans moved to the West,
they became farmers, cowboys, cattle ranchers,
or business owners. However, some African
Americans in the West still faced discrimination.

The Exodusters

A large group of African Americans from the South moved to the West. They became known as Exodusters. A man named Benjamin "Pap" Singleton was their leader. In the South, unfair laws kept African Americans from owning land and having the same rights as other Americans. Singleton discovered that Kansas was more open to African Americans having their own land. With his help, the Exodusters founded the African American community of Nicodemus (nik-oh-DEE-miss), Kansas, in 1877.

Benjamin "Pap" Singleton (left).
Exodusters gather on the main street
of Nicodemus, Kansas (below).

This is a view of
a stockyard in
the cattle town of
Abilene, Kansas,
in 1886.

Communities of the West

Throughout the West, pioneers formed
communities like Nicodemus. The communities
might be towns, **homesteads**, or camps,
depending on the type of work people did. Cattle
towns formed around railway stations. Cowboys
herded cattle to these towns. There, the animals
were sold to be used for meat and were put on
trains headed to stockyards in the East.

Gold miners settled in camps around the mines.

Gold miners were called forty-niners, because the gold rush started in 1849.

For homesteaders, the nearest neighbor might be several miles away. In order to feel a sense of community, homesteaders gathered with their neighbors for social events such as meetings or religious services.

Some people settled into camp communities where they lived in tents and shacks. If the number of people in a camp increased, a town would grow up around it.

A Clash of Ideas

Long before European settlers and pioneers arrived, Native Americans lived in many different parts of the country. The European settlers wanted to own the land, but Native Americans did not understand the idea of "owning" land. To them, it was impossible to own land. It would be like owning the sky or the ocean. Land became a major issue between settlers and Native Americans—especially in the West.

These chiefs are from the Piegan Blackfoot tribe, which is based in Montana.

Native American Communities

As more settlers arrived on the western **frontier** (frun-TEER), the demand for land grew. The U.S. government forced the Native American people who were living there to move. The Native people were sent to lands with poor soil that was difficult to farm. This caused them to become dependent on the government for food and supplies.

Native Americans were forced onto smaller and smaller areas of land.

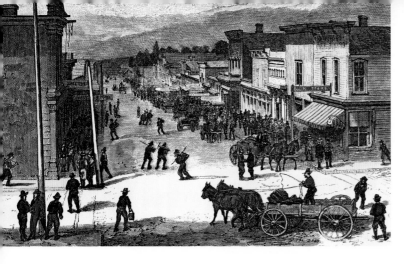

As towns grew, it became important to elect leaders and to pass laws that would keep people safe.

Frontier Laws and Government

As people began crowding into the frontier, there were no rules or laws. With so many people from different backgrounds now living together, there were all kinds of disagreements. To bring order, officials were elected to settle disputes, govern towns, and make laws. With this came the need for courts to enforce the laws and for law officers to capture criminals and protect the public. Sometimes, citizen groups would take on the job of law enforcement. They were called **vigilantes** (vih-juh-LAN-teez).

Cowboys and Cattle Ranches

Cattle ranches were built on large pieces of land. The ranches included a home for the rancher, barns, corrals, and stables. The ranchers hired cowboys to herd the cattle. Cowboys performed many other jobs on the ranch, too—from repairing buildings and fences to milking cows and caring for the horses.

The Rodeo

Cowboys competed in contests to show off their skills in riding, roping, and bronco busting (taming wild horses). These contests became known as rodeos, and they're still popular today.

The Roundup

In the spring and the fall, cowboys worked to bring in, or "round up," cattle from the open range. During a roundup, cowboys faced dangers such as falling off a horse and being dragged across the ground.

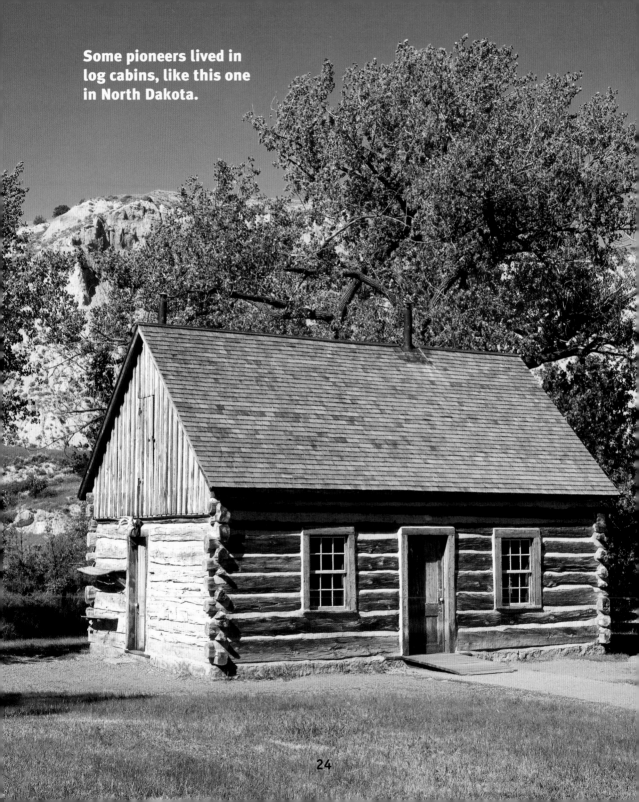

Some pioneers lived in log cabins, like this one in North Dakota.

CHAPTER 3

Life on the Frontier

When settlers arrived in the West, they had to learn new skills, such as how to build their own homes. With building homes and settling the land came long days filled with lots of work. All the members of a pioneer family had jobs to do. Despite the long and busy days, the pioneers found time for fun and entertainment.

Log cabins could be built with few tools, and no nails were needed!

Homes on the Range

In the West, the types of houses that were built depended on the **raw materials** that were available. Pioneers who settled near wooded areas cut down trees to build log cabins. On the wide-open prairie, there were few trees. Settlers in these areas stacked rectangular chunks of earth and grass called sod to build homes called soddies (SOD-eez). Soddies had dirt floors, few windows, and leaky roofs.

Sod homes were warm in the winter and cool in the summer.

Sod houses were full of bugs, mice, worms, and even snakes!

Settlers modeled their adobe homes after those of Native Americans of the Southwest.

In the deserts of the Southwest, settlers built homes with bricks made from adobe (uh-DOE-bee). Adobe is a mixture of clay and grass that is dried in the sun. Adobe homes stayed cool during the long, hot days in the desert. They were warm at night, when the desert was cold. Today, many houses in the Southwest are still made from adobe.

This adobe house is located in Santa Fe, New Mexico.

Native American Homes

Great Plains tribes, such as the Dakota and the Blackfoot, followed the bison herds. They hunted these animals for food and clothing. Since they were always on the move, these tribes built portable homes called tepees (TEE-peez). The Omaha, also of the Great Plains, used soil, grass, and tree branches to build homes called earth lodges. Tribes in the Northwest built large wooden homes called longhouses. Many families lived together in a single longhouse.

Some earth lodges housed several families—and their horses!

Buffalo chips are dried bison droppings.

This frontier woman and her child are gathering buffalo chips to use as fuel for the family's fire.

Women's Work

The settlers' days were filled with hard work. Women had many responsibilities, including raising children, cooking meals, storing food for winter, gardening, hauling water, and doing laundry. Women also stitched clothing and quilts, made candles and soap, prepared medicines, and cared for the sick or injured.

Cows were milked twice each day, once in the morning and again in the evening.

Home Work

Even children were expected to help their families with work. They milked cows, fed chickens, and gathered eggs and buffalo chips. Children also picked vegetables from the family garden. When boys were older and stronger, they helped their fathers chop wood and tend crops. Girls helped with cooking and caring for younger brothers or sisters.

School was closed during planting and harvesting times so children could help at home.

Education and Entertainment

School was held in one-room schoolhouses. One teacher taught all of the grades. There were few school supplies and books. Children wrote on **slates** instead of paper. They studied reading, spelling, handwriting, math, and history.

For fun, frontier families enjoyed playing cards and making music together. Sometimes neighbors would gather for dances or picnics. Children played games outdoors, swam, and made simple toys, such as dolls from dried cornhusks.

This example of a one-room schoolhouse shows students' desks and the heater (center) that provided warmth on cold winter days.

CHAPTER 4

Tough Times on the Prairie

People who settled on the prairie quickly learned the many challenges of life in their new home. They coped with rough weather, disease, and insects that destroyed their crops. When pioneers traveling west on the Oregon Trail first passed through the prairie, they thought the land couldn't be farmed. They mistakenly called the prairie the Great American Desert. But the prairie actually did offer good farmland and lots of open space.

Prairie windstorms could be so strong that covered wagons were blown over.

Mother Nature

Pioneers dealt with windstorms, blizzards, and tornadoes. Severe **droughts** (DROWTS) could kill their crops and leave them without food. Lightning strikes could set the prairie grasses on fire. These fires traveled quickly, destroying everything in their path. During the harsh winters, blowing snow could cover buildings, causing people to get lost as they walked from their homes to their barns.

Timeline of Settling the West

1840s
Pioneers begin moving west.

1848
James Marshall discovers gold at Sutter's Mill, California.

Health and Safety Concerns

Some years, millions of grasshoppers covered the prairies. They ate the crops, leaving little for the farmers to harvest. The grasshoppers ate the pioneers' straw hats, clothing, and fabrics. Pioneers also struggled with diseases, snake bites, and injuries from farming equipment. There were few doctors in the West, and medical care could be miles away. Many pioneers died from untreated diseases or infections.

1841–1866

500,000 people travel west on routes such as the Oregon Trail.

1862

Congress approves the Homestead Act.

John Deere's New Plow

Pioneer farmers had a hard time plowing the soil. Clumps of dirt would stick to the cast-iron plows they used. Farmers had to stop often to scrape the soil off of their plows. A man named John Deere invented a plow that solved this problem. Deere's plow had a blade made from smooth, polished steel and soil did not stick to it. John Deere went on to start a company that still makes farming equipment today.

John Deere (below, far right) shows farmers how his plow works.

Windmills and railroads made life easier for Western pioneers.

Making Life Easier

Several other new inventions made life easier for the pioneers. Farmers, especially, were helped by some of these, including barbed wire and windmills. Barbed wire is fencing with sharp points on it. Farmers used it to block off their land and protect their animals. Windmills helped farmers pump water from the ground more easily. And travel to the West became faster and easier when the first cross-country railroad was completed in 1869.

Western towns, ranches, and farms covered land that was once wilderness.

CHAPTER 5

The Impact of the Pioneers

The story of the pioneers settling the American West is one of excitement, survival, and adventure. But there is another side to the story. Western expansion forever changed the lives of Native Americans. They were forced off of the homelands that they had known for hundreds of years. The pioneer way of life also affected the land and the animals that lived on it.

 In 1890, a government report stated that there were no frontiers left to settle in the United States.

Effects on the Environment

Pioneers left their mark on the land in many ways. Those who settled in wooded areas cut down trees to use for building and for fuel. Some let their **livestock** graze until the grasses were gone. When pioneers cut and used plants, the homes and food sources for smaller creatures were sometimes destroyed. Hunting also killed many animals. However, when national parks were created, they helped preserve some of the Western lands.

Yellowstone National Park, located in present-day Wyoming, Montana, and Idaho, was the first national park in the world.

Bison were the major source of food and materials used for clothing and shelter by Native Americans of the Great Plains.

Changes for Native Americans

After Native Americans were forced to leave their homelands, their lives were never the same. Settlers turned the grasslands where bison once grazed into farms and ranches. This caused the bison to disappear. Tribes depended on the bison for food and skins. Pioneer hunters killed thousands of bison, leaving them to rot on the prairie. Without bison, Native Americans were left without their major food source.

Most of the men who traveled west with their families were farmers.

The American Spirit

The pioneers were determined to make their lives better, and they took many risks to reach this goal. During their travels, they faced new and difficult experiences in unfamiliar places. They learned how to build homes with new materials, grow food, make the things they needed, and survive harsh weather. Their bravery and sense of adventure helped build and grow the United States from coast to coast. ★

True Statistics

Size of land bought in the Louisiana Purchase:
828,800 square mi. (2,147,000 sq. km)

Number of states eventually carved out of
the Louisiana Purchase: 15

Number of people who traveled west on the Oregon
Trail from 1830 to 1870: About 500,000

Number of Europeans who moved to the American
West between 1830 and 1880: About 2 million

Year that gold was discovered in California: 1848

Year that the Homestead Act was signed: 1862

Size of a piece of land provided by the
Homestead Act: 160 acres (65 hectacres)

Number of African Americans who moved to Kansas
between 1865 and 1900: More than 15,000

Did you find the truth?

F The pioneers were the first people to settle the American West.

T Some early Western homes were made from dirt and grass.

Resources

Books

Bial, Raymond. *Frontier Settlements*. New York: Children's Press, 2004.

Burnett, Linda. *Pioneers: Adventure in a New Land*. New York: Children's Press, 2005.

Kalman, Bobbie. *Homes of the West*. New York: Crabtree Publishing Company, 1999.

Kamma, Anne. *If You Were a Pioneer on the Prairie*. New York: Scholastic, 2003.

Markel, Rita J. *Your Travel Guide to America's Old West*. Minneapolis: Lerner Publications Company, 2004.

Miller, Jay. *American Indian Families*. Danbury, CT: Children's Press, 1996.

Morley, Jacqueline. *You Wouldn't Want to Be an American Pioneer!: A Wilderness You'd Rather Not Tame*. New York: Franklin Watts, 2002.

Patent, Dorothy Hinshaw. *Homesteading: Settling America's Heartland*. New York: Walker, 1998.

Schlissel, Lillian. *Black Frontiers: A History of African American Heroes in the Old West*. New York: Simon & Schuster Books for Young Readers, 1995.

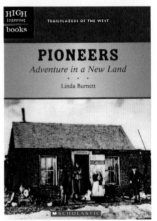

Organizations and Web Sites

California's Untold Stories: Gold Rush

www.museumca.org/goldrush/

Take a gold rush quiz and read about the people who journeyed to California to search for gold.

Kidinfo: Pioneers and Westward Expansion

www.kidinfo.com/American_History/Pioneers.html

Read about a variety of topics related to westward expansion.

PBS: The West

www.pbs.org/weta/thewest/program/episodes/five/cowboys.htm

Find out more about the lives of real cowboys.

Places to Visit

Autry National Center: Museum of the American West

Griffith Park Campus
Autry National Center
4700 Western Heritage Way
Los Angeles, CA 90027-1462
(323) 667-2000
www.autrynationalcenter.org/visit.php
View art and artifacts from the American West.

The Museum of Westward Expansion

11 North 4th Street
St. Louis, MO 63102
(314) 655-1700
www.nps.gov/archive/jeff/expansion_museum.html
Explore the history of the West through exhibits about Lewis and Clark, Native Americans, the pioneers, and more.

Important Words

claim – a demand for something as one's right

corrals – a fenced area that holds horses, cattle, or other animals

discriminated (diss-KRIM-uh-nate-id) – judged or treated unfairly because of race, religion, gender, or other factors

droughts (DROWTS)– long periods with little rain or very dry weather

frontier (frun-TEER)– the edge of a region that is mostly unsettled by people

homesteads – pieces of land given by the government to settlers

immigrants (IH-muh-grints)– people who move to another country from their native land

livestock – animals raised on a farm or ranch, such as horses, sheep, and cows

pioneers – those who are the first in a culture to explore or live in a place

raw materials – a natural substance that is made into a useful finished product. For example, trees were cut down and turned into lumber to construct buildings.

slates – tablets made of thin, blue-gray rock that were used for writing

vigilantes (vih-juh-LAN-teez) – those who seek to punish a criminal without legal authority

Index

Page numbers in **bold** indicate illustrations

About the Author

Teresa Domnauer is the author of many nonfiction books for children. She has a bachelor's degree in creative writing from Emerson College and received her teaching certification from Ohio Dominican University. Ms. Domnauer lives in Connecticut with her husband, Brendon, and their two daughters, Ellie and Robin.